THE 18 GREAT STEP TO ENTREPRENEURIAL SUCCESS

EMMANUEL AMAGADA

CONTENTS

Title Page
Introduction
CHAPTER 1: DEVELOPING A CLEAR BUSINESS PLAN   1
CHAPTER 2: IDENTIFYING AND UNDERSTANDING YOUR TARGET MARKET   7
CHAPTER 3: NETWORKING AND BUILDING RELATIONSHIPS   9
CHAPTER 4: CONDUCTING MARKET RESEARCH AND ANALYSIS   12
CHAPTER 5: FINDING AND SECURING FUNDING SOURCES   15
CHAPTER 6: FINDING AND SECURING FUNDING SOURCES   18
CHAPTER 7: HIRING AND MANAGING EMPLOYEES   21
CHAPTER 8: MANAGING FINANCES AND CASH FLOW   24
CHAPTER 9 STAYING ORGANIZED AND EFFICIENT   28
CHAPTER 10 CONTINUOUSLY LEARNING AND ADAPTING   32
CHAPTER 11: SETTING AND ACHIEVING GOALS   34
CHAPTER 12: BUILDING A STRONG TEAM   37
CHAPTER 13: DEVELOPING EFFECTIVE MARKETING STRATEGIES   40
CHAPTER 14: UNDERSTANDING AND COMPLYING WITH LEGAL AND REGULATORY REQUIREMENTS   43
CHAPTER 15: MANAGING RISK AND UNCERTAINTY   46

CHAPTER 16: LEVERAGING TECHNOLOGY AND AUTOMATION	50
CHAPTER 17: LEVERAGING TECHNOLOGY AND AUTOMATION	53
CHAPTER 18: MEASURING AND EVALUATING SUCCESS AND PROGRESS	57
BONUS POINT	61
SUMMARY	68
About The Author	71
Books By This Author	73

INTRODUCTION

The 18 significant measures to accomplish entrepreneurial triumph is a guide that encompasses the fundamental strides to reaching victory as a businessperson. The guide includes subjects such as crafting an explicit business scheme, identifying the target market, establishing a network, conducting market research, discovering funding sources, creating a powerful brand, employing and administering staff, managing finances, maintaining organization, consistently learning, setting and accomplishing objectives, building an efficacious team, devising practical marketing strategies, comprehending legal and regulatory prerequisites, managing hazards, exploiting technology, preserving a constructive outlook, and assessing and gauging success. The guide aspires to furnish entrepreneurs with the instruments and methods that are indispensable to commence and expand a flourishing enterprise. Additionally, the guide concentrates on providing pragmatic and applicable recommendations for businesspeople at all stages of their business odyssey. It covers indispensable topics such as devising a business scheme, recognizing the target market, establishing a network, conducting market research, discovering funding sources, creating a powerful brand, employing and administering staff, managing finances, maintaining organization, consistently learning, setting and accomplishing objectives, building an efficacious team, devising practical marketing strategies, comprehending legal and regulatory prerequisites, managing hazards, exploiting technology, preserving a constructive outlook, and assessing and gauging success. The guide is engineered to be an all-encompassing resource that can be utilized by businesspeople of all experience levels, from those just starting out to those who are looking to ascend their enterprise to the next echelon. Furthermore, the guide also deals with the significance of preserving a constructive mentality and outlook throughout the entrepreneurial expedition. Embarking on a business enterprise can be an arduous and nerve-wracking procedure, and it is indispensable to preserve a constructive mentality and remain stimulated. The guide also incorporates data on how to manage hazards and unpredictability, which is an inescapable element of launching and enlarging a business. The guide provides worthwhile insights on how to manage finances, cash flow, and scrutinize advancement and success. The guide also accentuates the significance of keeping up-to-date with legal and regulatory prerequisites. It can be overpowering for businesspeople to steer the legal side of starting a business, but this guide provides pragmatic guidance on how to remain obedient and circumvent any legal issues. The 18 significant measures to accomplish entrepreneurial triumph is an invaluable resource for anybody seeking to begin or expand a business.

It envelops all the critical strides and methods that businesspeople need to apprehend to be successful and provides applicable and pragmatic guidance that can be executed immediately.

CHAPTER 1: DEVELOPING A CLEAR BUSINESS PLAN

A business plan is a document that outlines the goals and objectives of a business, as well as the strategies and actions that will be taken to achieve those goals. It is a crucial first step in starting a new business and is often required by investors and lenders as part of the decision-making process.

A clear and well-written business plan can help entrepreneurs in several ways. It serves as a roadmap for the business, outlining the steps that need to be taken to achieve success. It also helps entrepreneurs to identify potential challenges and obstacles, and to develop strategies for overcoming them. Additionally, a business plan can help entrepreneurs to secure funding from investors or lenders, as it provides a detailed overview of the business and its financial projections.

There are several key components of a business plan, including:

- Executive Summary: A brief overview of the business and its key objectives
- Company Description: A detailed description of the business, including its mission, values, and goals
- Industry Analysis: An analysis of the industry in which the business will operate, including market trends and competitors
- Market Analysis: A detailed analysis of the target market, including demographics, buying habits, and potential customers
- Sales and Marketing Strategy: A description of the strategies and tactics that will be used to reach and engage customers
- Service or Product Line: A description of the products or services that the business will offer

- Financial Projections: Detailed financial projections, including revenue, expenses, and profit projections

Illustration: A business plan can be visualized as a blueprint for building a house. Just like how a blueprint includes the design and layout of the house, the materials that will be used, and the construction process, a business plan includes the details of the business, the market and competition, the strategies and actions that will be taken, and the financial projections.

A clear and well-written business plan is essential for entrepreneurs who are starting a new business. It serves as a roadmap for the business, helps to identify potential challenges and obstacles, and can be used to secure funding from investors or lenders. By including all the key components of a business plan, entrepreneurs can ensure that their business has the best chance of success.

NOTE:

Developing a clear business plan is essential for any entrepreneur who wants to start or grow a successful business. A business plan is a roadmap that outlines your business's objectives, strategies, and tactics, and it helps you identify potential challenges and opportunities. A well-developed business plan will also help you secure funding and attract investors, as well as guide your decision-making process as your business evolves.

To develop a clear business plan, you should follow these steps:

Define your business concept: Start by clearly defining your business concept. This should include what products or services you will offer, who your target market is, and how you will differentiate yourself from your competitors.

Conduct market research: Before you launch your business, you need to conduct thorough market research to understand your industry, target market, and competition. This will help you identify your unique selling proposition and develop a marketing strategy that resonates with your target audience.

Determine your business structure: You need to decide on the legal structure of your business, such as a sole proprietorship, partnership, LLC, or corporation. Each structure has its advantages and disadvantages, and you should choose the one that best suits your business goals and risk tolerance.

Develop a financial plan: You need to create a detailed financial plan that includes your startup costs, revenue projections, and cash flow analysis. This will help you determine how much funding you need to start and run your business, and it will guide your financial decisions as your business grows.

Create a marketing plan: Your marketing plan should outline how you will promote your business and attract customers. This should include your branding strategy, social media strategy, advertising plan, and other tactics you will use to reach your target audience.

Develop an operational plan: Your operational plan should outline how you will manage the day-to-day operations of your business. This should include staffing, inventory management, production processes
, and any other operational procedures that are necessary for your business to function smoothly.

Set goals and milestones: You should set clear goals and milestones for your business, such as revenue targets, customer acquisition goals, or product development milestones. This will help you track your progress and make adjustments to your business strategy as needed.

Identify potential challenges and risks: As you develop your business plan, you should identify potential challenges and risks that your business may face. This could include changes in the market, economic downturns, or legal and regulatory issues. Identifying these risks ahead of time will help you develop contingency plans and mitigate their impact on your business.

Get feedback and revise your plan: Once you have developed a draft business plan, it's important to get feedback from trusted advisors, mentors, or industry experts. Incorporate their feedback into your plan and revise it accordingly.

By following these steps, you can develop a clear and comprehensive business plan that will help you achieve your business goals and navigate the challenges of entrepreneurship. Remember that your business plan should be a living document that you revise and update as your business evolves.

Include an executive summary: Your business plan should include an executive summary that provides an overview of your business plan. This should highlight the key points of your plan, such as your business concept, target market, financial projections, and marketing strategy.

Provide a company description: You should provide a detailed description of your company, including its history, mission statement, and values. This will help investors and other stakeholders understand what your company stands for and what it hopes to achieve.

Outline your products or services: Your business plan should provide a detailed description of the products or services you will offer, including their features and benefits. This will help potential customers understand what your business has to offer and how it can solve their needs or problems.

Include a competitive analysis: You should conduct a competitive analysis that identifies your main competitors, their strengths and weaknesses, and how you will differentiate yourself from them. This will help you understand the competitive landscape and develop strategies to gain a competitive advantage.

Provide a management and staffing plan: Your business plan should outline your management team and staffing plan. This should include their qualifications, roles and responsibilities, and how you plan to recruit and retain employees.

Include a funding request: If you are seeking funding for your business, your business plan should include a funding request that outlines how much funding you need and how you plan to use it. This should be supported by your financial projections and cash flow analysis.

By including these elements in your business plan, you can create a comprehensive and effective roadmap for your business that will help you achieve your goals and succeed in your industry.

Provide financial projections: Your business plan should include financial projections that estimate your revenue, expenses, and profits over the next few years. This will help you and potential investors understand the financial viability of your business and the potential return on investment.

Develop a risk management plan: Your business plan should include a risk management plan that identifies potential risks and outlines strategies to mitigate them. This should include contingency plans for events such as economic downturns, natural disasters, or changes in the market.

Include legal and regulatory compliance: Your business plan should include information on any legal and regulatory requirements for your industry, such as permits, licenses, and taxes. This will ensure that your business is compliant with all applicable laws and regulations.

Develop a timeline: Your business plan should include a timeline that outlines key milestones and deadlines for achieving your goals. This will help you stay on track and ensure that you are making progress towards your objectives.

Review and revise regularly: Your business plan should be reviewed and revised regularly to ensure that it remains relevant and effective. This will help you adapt to changes in the market and make necessary adjustments to your business strategy.

Developing a clear business plan is essential for any entrepreneur who wants to start or grow a successful business. By following these steps, you can create a comprehensive and effective roadmap for your business that will help you achieve your goals and succeed in your industry.

CHAPTER 2: IDENTIFYING AND UNDERSTANDING YOUR TARGET MARKET

One of the key steps in achieving entrepreneurial success is identifying and understanding your target market. This involves researching and analysing the demographics, habits, and needs of the customers you hope to reach with your business. By understanding your target market, you can make informed decisions about your product or service offerings, marketing strategies, and overall business direction.

To begin identifying your target market, start by considering the following questions:

- Who are your potential customers?
- What is their age, gender, income level, education level, and location?
- What are their interests and hobbies?
- What are their pain points and needs?
- What motivates them to make a purchase?

Answering these questions will help you to create a clear and detailed profile of your target market. For example, if you are selling a new type of workout equipment, your target market may be individuals who are interested in fitness, have disposable income, and are looking for an effective way to get in shape.

Once you have a clear picture of your target market, you can use this information to make strategic decisions about your business. For example, you may choose to focus your marketing efforts on social media platforms that are popular among your target market, or you may decide to offer a warranty or guarantee that addresses a specific pain point or concern that your target market has.

there are additional steps that can be taken to further understand

and segment your target market.

One such step is conducting market research. This can include surveys, focus groups, and interviews with potential customers to gather more in-depth information about their needs, preferences, and buying habits. Market research can also include analysing data from industry reports and competitors. This will give you a better understanding of the current market conditions and trends and help you identify opportunities for your business.

Another step is to segment your target market. This means breaking down your target market into smaller groups based on specific characteristics or behaviours. For example, you might segment your target market by age, income, or location. By segmenting your target market, you can create more targeted marketing campaigns and tailored product or service offerings that will appeal to specific groups within your target market.

Additionally, you can track the progress and customer engagement in your target market by creating customer personas. These are fictional characters that represent your ideal customer based on the research you have conducted. It allows you to keep track of your customer's behaviour, preferences and demographics and also helps in creating a customer-centric approach to your business.

Overall, the key to successfully identifying and understanding your target market is to continuously gather and analyse data, and make adjustments to your business strategies as needed. It's a dynamic process that requires ongoing effort and adaptation.

By taking the time to identify and understand your target market, you can ensure that your business is well-positioned to meet the needs of your customers and achieve entrepreneurial success.

CHAPTER 3: NETWORKING AND BUILDING RELATIONSHIPS

Networking and building relationships are crucial aspects of entrepreneurial success. By developing a strong network of contacts, entrepreneurs can gain access to valuable resources, knowledge, and opportunities that can help them grow their business. In this chapter, we will discuss the key points and examples of how to effectively network and build relationships as an entrepreneur.

Key Points:

Key Point 1: Networking is about building connections and relationships, not just handing out business cards.

Networking is an essential aspect of building a successful business, but it's not just about handing out business cards to as many people as possible. It's about building connections and relationships with people who can help you achieve your goals and vice versa. Rather than just collecting a pile of business cards, focus on building meaningful relationships with people who can provide valuable resources, knowledge, and opportunities that can help you grow your business. This approach will help you to build a network of contacts that are genuinely interested in your business and are more likely to be supportive and helpful in the future.

Key Point 2: Focus on building relationships with people who can help you achieve your goals and vice versa.

When networking, it's important to focus on building relationships with people who can help you achieve your goals and vice versa. This means identifying individuals or organizations that can provide valuable resources, knowledge, or opportunities that align with your business goals. For example, if your goal is to increase sales, it would be beneficial to connect with individuals or organizations that have a large customer base or influence in your target market. By building relationships with these individuals or organizations, you'll be able to tap into their resources and influence to help grow your business. Additionally, it's important to look for opportunities to help and support others in your network as well, as this can help build trust and long-lasting relationships.

Key Point 3: Attend networking events, join professional organizations, and utilize online networking tools to expand your network.

Expanding your network is crucial for entrepreneurial success, and there are many ways to do this. One effective method is to attend networking events, such as business conferences, trade shows, and networking groups. These events provide a platform for entrepreneurs to connect with other business owners, potential clients, and other industry professionals. Joining professional organizations, such as trade associations or industry groups, can also be a great way to expand your network and connect with others in your field.

Another effective way to expand your network is to utilize online networking tools, such as LinkedIn, Twitter, or Facebook. These tools allow you to connect with a wider range of people and expand your reach beyond your immediate geographic area. By actively engaging with others on these platforms, you can build relationships with potential clients, partners, and other industry professionals. You can also use these platforms to share your expertise and knowledge, making it more likely that others will want to connect and work with you.

Overall, attending networking events, joining professional

organizations, and utilizing online networking tools are great ways to expand your network and connect with others who can help you achieve your goals.

Key Point 4: Follow up with contacts regularly to maintain the relationship and stay top-of-mind.

Networking is not a one-time event, it's an ongoing process. Even if you've made a great connection with someone at a networking event, it doesn't mean that the relationship will automatically continue to grow. To maintain and strengthen the relationships you've built, it's important to follow up with your contacts regularly. This can include sending an email or LinkedIn message, scheduling a phone call, or even meeting up for coffee or lunch.

By following up, you'll be able to keep the conversation going and stay top-of-mind with your contacts. This will make it more likely that they will think of you when an opportunity arises that aligns with your goals. Additionally, by staying in touch, you'll be able to build deeper connections and trust with your contacts, which is essential for long-term relationship building.

It's also important to remember that following up does not always have to be about business, you can also check in for a personal catch up and make sure you maintain a balance.

Following up with your contacts regularly is an important step in maintaining and strengthening the relationships you've built through networking. By staying top-of-mind and building deeper connections, you'll be more likely to secure valuable resources, knowledge, and opportunities that can help you grow your business.

CHAPTER 4: CONDUCTING MARKET RESEARCH AND ANALYSIS

Market research and analysis is a crucial step in the entrepreneurial process. It involves gathering, analysing, and interpreting data about your target market, competitors, and industry to inform your business decisions. By conducting market research, you can gain a better understanding of your customers, identify new opportunities, and make more informed decisions about your product or service offerings.

Key Points:

1. Understand Your Target Market: One of the most important aspects of market research is understanding your target market. This includes identifying their demographics, needs, wants, and pain points. This information can be used to develop effective marketing strategies and create products or services that meet the specific needs of your target market.
2. Analyse Your Competitors: Understanding your competitors is also crucial. This includes analysing their products, services, pricing, marketing strategies, and overall business model. This information can be used to identify areas where you can differentiate your business and gain a competitive advantage.
3. Assess Industry Trends: Keeping up-to-date with industry trends is important. This includes understanding the current state of the market, identifying any upcoming changes or disruptions, and determining which trends are likely to have the most impact on your business.
4. Determine the size of the market: Understanding the size of the market is also important. This includes

assessing the total market size, growth rate, and potential for future growth. This information can be used to determine the potential revenue and profitability of your business.
5. Identify customer needs and behaviour: Market research can also help you to understand your customers' needs and behaviour. This includes identifying their purchasing habits, decision-making processes, and what motivates them to buy a product or service. This information can be used to create effective marketing campaigns and improve the customer experience.
6. Use different methods for market research: There are different methods for conducting market research, including surveys, focus groups, interviews, and secondary research. Each method has its own advantages and disadvantages and it is important to choose the best method for your specific research needs.

Examples:
1. A start-up company that sells organic food products can conduct market research by surveying their target market to understand their needs, preferences, and pain points. This information can be used to develop products and packaging that align with their target market's values and preferences.
2. A business that wants to enter into a new market can conduct market research by analysing their competitors' products, services, and pricing. This information can be used to identify gaps in the market and develop a pricing strategy that is competitive and profitable.
3. A business that wants to stay competitive in the market can conduct market research by assessing industry trends. For example, understanding that there is an increasing trend in e-commerce, they can start to

implement strategies and plans to move their business online, or provide online ordering or delivery service.
4. A business that wants to enter into a new market can conduct market research to determine the size of the market. For example, by conducting a survey, they can find out that there are 100,000 potential customers in the area and the market is growing at a rate of 10% per year, which can help them to determine their revenue potential and make informed decisions about their business.
5. A business that sells a new type of technology product can conduct market research by identifying customer needs and behaviour. For example, by conducting interviews with potential customers, they can find out that their target market is primarily made up of tech-savvy millennials who are motivated to buy the product because of its convenience and ease of use.

A business that wants to understand its target market can conduct market research by using different methods. For example, they can conduct a survey to gather general information about the target market, and then conduct focus groups to gain deeper insights into their needs, wants, and pain points.

Market research and analysis is an essential step in the entrepreneurial process. It helps entrepreneurs to gain valuable insights and information that can inform their business decisions, improve their products and services, and increase their chances of success in the market.

CHAPTER 5: FINDING AND SECURING FUNDING SOURCES

Entrepreneurship often requires a significant investment of time and money, and securing funding is a crucial step in the process of starting and growing a business. There are several different funding options available, each with its own set of advantages and disadvantages.

1. Key points:
2. Understand the different types of funding: There are several types of funding available, including angel investing, venture capital, crowdfunding, grants, and loans. Each type has its own set of requirements, advantages, and disadvantages.
3. Create a solid business plan: A well-written business plan is essential when seeking funding. It should clearly outline the business's goals, strategies, and financial projections.
4. Network, network, network: Building relationships and networking with potential investors, lenders, and other entrepreneurs can help to increase the chances of securing funding.
5. Be prepared to give up equity: Many funding options, such as venture capital and angel investing, require entrepreneurs to give up a portion of the ownership of their company in exchange for funding.
6. Consider alternative funding options: Crowdfunding, grants, and loans from the government or non-profits are alternative funding options that may be more accessible for some entrepreneurs.
7. Leverage your personal and professional connections: Personal and professional connections can be a valuable resource when seeking funding. Reach out to family

members, friends, mentors, and industry contacts to see if they are willing to invest in your business.

8. Be transparent and honest with potential investors: Investors want to see a clear and realistic picture of your business and its potential for growth. Be transparent about the current state of your business, any challenges or risks you may be facing, and your plans for the future.
9. Do your due diligence: Research potential investors and funding options thoroughly before committing to any agreements. Make sure you fully understand the terms and conditions of any funding agreements and that they align with your business goals.
10. Have a Plan B: It's important to have a backup plan in case your primary funding options fall through. Consider alternative funding sources, such as small business loans or credit lines, and have a plan in place to manage cash flow in the short term.
11. Be aware of the tax implications: Each funding option has its own set of tax implications that entrepreneurs need to be aware of. For example, equity funding may result in a capital gain or loss, while debt funding may have tax implications for interest payments. It's important to consult with a tax advisor to understand the potential tax implications of different funding options.
12. Keep track of your progress: Keep detailed records of the funding options you've explored, the contacts you've made, and the progress you've made in securing funding. This will help you stay organized and be better prepared when presenting your business plan to potential investors.
13. Be patient: Securing funding can be a time-consuming process, and it may take longer than expected to secure the funding you need. It's important to be patient and persistent in your efforts.

Examples:
1. A start-up company that creates eco-friendly products, secures funding from a venture capital firm in exchange for a 20% equity in the company.
2. A small business owner seeking to expand their brick-and-mortar store, successfully raises funds through a crowdfunding campaign by offering rewards to backers such as discounts and exclusive merchandise.
3. A social enterprise that aims to provide education to underprivileged children, receives a grant from a non-profit organization to help cover operational costs and expand their reach.

Securing funding is a critical step in the process of starting and growing a business, and entrepreneurs need to be aware of the different funding options available, the tax implications, and the progress they are making. It is important to be prepared, network, be transparent and honest, have a plan B, and to keep track of progress. Entrepreneurs should also be aware that the funding process takes time and be patient, persistent in their efforts to secure funding.

CHAPTER 6: FINDING AND SECURING FUNDING SOURCES

Entrepreneurs need capital to start and grow their businesses. Finding and securing funding sources is a crucial step in the entrepreneurial journey. There are several options available to entrepreneurs, including traditional bank loans, crowdfunding, angel investing, and venture capital.

Key Point: Identifying the right funding source for your business is important as it will depend on your business needs and goals, your personal financial situation, and the stage of development of your business.

1. Traditional Bank Loans: One of the most common funding sources for entrepreneurs is traditional bank loans. Banks offer a variety of loan options, such as term loans, line of credit, and SBA loans. To qualify for a bank loan, entrepreneurs typically need to have a solid business plan, good credit history, and collateral.

Example: A small business owner needs to purchase new equipment to expand their production capacity. They apply for a term loan from their local bank, providing their business plan, financial statements, and collateral (such as real estate or equipment) as collateral for the loan.

2. Crowdfunding: Another funding option for entrepreneurs is crowdfunding. Crowdfunding is a way to raise money from a large number of people, typically through an online platform. Entrepreneurs can use crowdfunding to raise money for a specific project or idea, and offer rewards or perks to those who contribute.

Example: A musician wants to record their first album but lacks the funds to do so. They create a crowdfunding campaign on a popular platform like Kickstarter. They set a funding goal and offer rewards such as autographed CDs or VIP concert experiences to those who contribute.

3. Angel Investing: Angel investors are wealthy individuals who provide capital to start-ups in exchange for equity in the company. Angel investors typically have experience in the industry in which the start-up operates and can also provide mentorship and guidance to the entrepreneur.

Example: A tech start-up has developed a new software that streamlines the logistics process for e-commerce businesses. They pitch their idea to an angel investor who has experience in the e-commerce industry. The angel investor is impressed by the potential of the software and decides to invest in the company in exchange for a percentage of ownership.

4. Venture Capital: Venture capital firms provide funding to start-ups that have a high potential for growth and returns. Venture capital firms typically invest in more established companies that have a proven track record and a scalable business model.

Example: A biotech start-up has developed a new drug that has shown promising results in early clinical trials. They pitch their idea to a venture capital firm that specializes in biotech investments. The venture capital firm is impressed by the potential of the drug and decides to invest in the company in exchange for a percentage of ownership.

Another funding option for entrepreneurs is government grants. Government grants are funds provided by government agencies to support specific business activities or industries. These grants are typically awarded to businesses that meet certain criteria and can be used for specific purposes such as research and development, marketing and export, or hiring and training employees.

Example: A renewable energy start-up has developed a new

technology for generating electricity from waste. They apply for a grant from the Department of Energy to support the commercialization of their technology. The grant is awarded to the start-up and they use the funds to build a pilot plant and conduct further research.

Additionally, it's worth mentioning that a combination of funding sources can also be used to support a business. For example, a start-up may use crowdfunding to raise initial funds and then secure a bank loan to expand their operations, or a small business owner may use a line of credit to manage cash flow and then secure an angel investment to develop a new product line.

Another option that is becoming more popular is bootstrapping, it's a way of funding a business using personal savings or credit card debt. Bootstrapping allows entrepreneurs to start a business with very little investment and keep full ownership of their business.

Example: A graphic designer starts a web design business with very little money. She uses her own savings to purchase a computer, software, and other equipment she needs. She also takes out a small loan to cover rent and other expenses. Over time, as the business grows, she is able to reinvest the profits back into the business and expand her offerings.

There are many different funding options available to entrepreneurs and the right one will depend on your business needs and goals, your personal financial situation, and the stage of development of your business. It's important to do your research and consider multiple options, as well as to have a solid financial plan and a clear vision for the future of your business to increase your chances of success in finding and securing funding.

CHAPTER 7: HIRING AND MANAGING EMPLOYEES

Hiring and managing employees is a crucial aspect of running a successful business. A business owner must be able to attract, hire, and retain talented employees to help the business grow. Additionally, it is important to establish effective management practices to ensure that employees are productive and motivated.

Key Points:

- Clearly define job roles and responsibilities: Before hiring employees, it is important to define the specific duties and responsibilities for each position. This will help to attract the right candidates and ensure that employees understand what is expected of them.
- Develop a thorough recruitment process: A thorough recruitment process will help to attract the best candidates for the job. This process should include advertising the position, reviewing resumes and conducting interviews, and assessing qualifications and skills.
- Establish a positive work culture: A positive work culture is essential for employee motivation and retention. A business owner should strive to create an environment that is inclusive, respectful, and supportive.
- Implement effective management practices: Effective management practices include setting clear goals and expectations, providing regular feedback, and fostering open communication. Additionally, it is important to provide regular training and development opportunities to help employees grow and succeed.
- Provide incentives and rewards: Providing incentives

and rewards can help to motivate employees and improve performance. This can include bonuses, profit-sharing, and employee recognition programs.
- Establish clear communication channels: Clear and open communication is essential for effective management. A business owner should establish channels for employees to share ideas and feedback, and encourage regular meetings to discuss progress and address any concerns.
- Manage performance and conduct regular evaluations: Regular evaluations of employee performance are important for identifying areas for improvement and providing feedback. A business owner should establish clear performance metrics, and hold regular performance reviews to discuss progress and set goals for the future.
- Address and resolve conflicts: Conflict is an inevitable part of any workplace. A business owner should be equipped to address and resolve conflicts in a timely and effective manner. This can involve providing mediation, implementing policies and procedures, or taking disciplinary action if necessary.

Examples:
- A small retail business owner clearly defines job roles and responsibilities for sales associates, cashiers, and managers. This helps to attract the right candidates and ensures that employees understand their specific duties.
- A startup founder establishes a thorough recruitment process that includes advertising the position, reviewing resumes, conducting interviews, and assessing qualifications and skills. This helps to attract the best candidates for the job.
- A software company owner creates a positive work culture by fostering open communication, providing regular training and development opportunities, and encouraging employee feedback. This helps to keep

employees motivated and engaged.
- A marketing agency owner implements effective management practices by setting clear goals and expectations, providing regular feedback, and fostering open communication. This helps to ensure that employees are productive and motivated.

Examples:
- A manufacturing company provides incentives and rewards to employees who meet or exceed production targets. This helps to improve performance and boost productivity.
- A consulting firm establishes regular team meetings to encourage open communication and feedback. This helps to ensure that employees feel heard and valued.
- A restaurant owner conducts regular performance evaluations to assess employee performance and identify areas for improvement. This helps to ensure that employees are meeting expectations and contributing to the success of the business.
- A web development company has a clear process for addressing and resolving conflicts. This include providing mediation, implementing policies and procedures, or taking disciplinary action if necessary, which helps to maintain a positive work environment.

Hiring and managing employees is a critical aspect of running a successful business. By clearly defining job roles and responsibilities, developing a thorough recruitment process, establishing a positive work culture, and implementing effective management practices, a business owner can attract, hire, and retain talented employees, and ensure that they are productive and motivated.

CHAPTER 8: MANAGING FINANCES AND CASH FLOW

Managing finances and cash flow is a crucial aspect of entrepreneurial success. This includes understanding and monitoring your income and expenses, forecasting future cash flow, and making smart financial decisions. In this chapter, we will cover key points and provide examples to help you effectively manage your finances and cash flow.

Key Point 1: Understand and Monitor Your Income and Expenses

It is essential to have a clear understanding of your income and expenses to effectively manage your finances. This includes tracking all incoming revenue and outgoing expenses, such as rent, employee salaries, and inventory costs. By regularly reviewing this information, you will be able to identify areas where you can cut costs and increase revenue.

Example: A small retail business tracks their income and expenses and realizes they are spending a significant amount of money on inventory that is not selling. They make adjustments to their inventory purchasing and see an increase in cash flow as a result.

Key Point 2: Forecast Future Cash Flow

Forecasting future cash flow involves predicting how much money you will have coming in and going out in the future. This helps you to anticipate any potential financial challenges and make plans to address them.

Example: A startup company creates a cash flow forecast for the next 12 months and predicts that they will have a shortage of funds in the third quarter. They use this information to secure additional funding before the shortage occurs.

Key Point 3: Make Smart Financial Decisions

Making smart financial decisions involves considering the long-term financial health of your business, rather than just focusing on short-term gains. This includes evaluating investment opportunities, setting realistic budgets, and avoiding unnecessary risks.

Example: A business owner is presented with the opportunity to invest in a new product line. They conduct market research and a financial analysis and determine that the potential return on investment is not worth the risk, so they decide not to pursue it.

Key Point 4: Manage Debt and Credit

Managing debt and credit is an important part of financial management for entrepreneurs. This includes understanding the types of debt and credit available to your business, and how to use them effectively. It also means being aware of the interest rates, terms and conditions, and the potential impact on your cash flow.

Example: A business owner takes out a loan to purchase new equipment for their company. They carefully review the terms and interest rates of the loan and create a repayment plan that fits within their projected cash flow. By managing the debt responsibly, they are able to improve the efficiency and productivity of their business.

Key Point 5: Keep Accurate Financial Records

Keeping accurate financial records is crucial for effective financial management. This includes maintaining detailed records of all income and expenses, as well as any loans or investments. Accurate records will allow you to easily track your business's performance, prepare for tax season, and make informed financial decisions.

Example: A small business owner sets up a system for tracking income and expenses and regularly updates it. As a result, they have accurate financial records and are able to easily identify areas where they can cut costs and increase revenue.

In summary, managing finances and cash flow is a critical

aspect of entrepreneurial success. It involves understanding and monitoring your income and expenses, forecasting future cash flow, making smart financial decisions, managing debt and credit, and keeping accurate financial records. By staying on top of your finances and making informed decisions, you can ensure the long-term financial health of your business.

Key Point 6: Create a Budget and Stick to It

Creating a budget and sticking to it is a crucial step in managing finances and cash flow. A budget will help you understand where your money is going and identify areas where you can reduce costs. Once you have created a budget, it is important to stick to it as closely as possible.

Example: A restaurant owner creates a budget for food and labor costs. By sticking to the budget, they are able to keep costs low and increase their profit margins.

Key Point 7: Use Financial Tools and Software

There are many financial tools and software available that can help you manage your finances and cash flow more effectively. These include accounting software, budgeting software, and invoicing software. These tools can automate many of the financial tasks, making it easier for you to track your income and expenses, and forecast future cash flow.

Example: A business owner uses accounting software to track income and expenses, create invoices and financial reports, and forecast future cash flow. This allows them to easily monitor their financial performance and make informed decisions.

Managing finances and cash flow is an essential aspect of entrepreneurial success. It involves understanding and monitoring your income and expenses, forecasting future cash flow, making smart financial decisions, managing debt and credit, keeping accurate financial records, creating a budget and sticking to it, and using financial tools and software. By staying on top of your finances and making informed decisions, you can ensure the long-term financial health of your business.

CHAPTER 9 STAYING ORGANIZED AND EFFICIENT

One key to entrepreneurial success is staying organized and efficient in all aspects of your business. This includes everything from managing your time and tasks, to keeping accurate records and financials, to maintaining a clean and functional workspace. By staying organized, you can ensure that your business runs smoothly and that you are able to focus on what is most important - growing your business and achieving your goals.

Here are some key points to consider when staying organized and efficient in your business:

1. Time management - One of the most important things you can do to stay organized is to manage your time effectively. This includes setting clear goals and priorities, creating a schedule and sticking to it, and using tools and apps to help you stay on track.
2. Task management - In addition to managing your time, you also need to manage your tasks effectively. This includes breaking down larger tasks into smaller, manageable chunks, creating a to-do list, and using tools and apps to help you stay organized and on top of your responsibilities.
3. Record keeping - Keeping accurate records is essential for any business. This includes keeping track of your finances, inventory, customer information, and more. Use of tools like CRM, accounting software, inventory management software will help you keep your records up to date and easily accessible.
4. Financial management - Financial management is also an important aspect of staying organized. This includes creating a budget, keeping accurate financial records,

and monitoring your cash flow. You should also make sure to regularly review your financials and make adjustments as needed.
5. Workspace organization - A cluttered and disorganized workspace can be distracting and unproductive. Keep your workspace clean and organized by regularly decluttering, using storage solutions, and creating a functional layout.
6. Automation - Automation is a great way to save time and stay organized. There are a variety of tools and apps available that can help automate various tasks and processes, such as email marketing, invoicing, and more.

By following these key points, you can stay organized and efficient in your business. This will help you save time and energy, focus on what's important, and ultimately achieve greater success as an entrepreneur.

7. Prioritization - Prioritization is an essential part of staying organized and efficient. It involves identifying the most important tasks and activities that need to be done and focusing on them first. This allows you to focus your time and energy on what is most important, rather than wasting time on less important or unnecessary tasks.
8. Delegation - As an entrepreneur, it is important to recognize that you cannot do everything on your own. Delegation is a key aspect of staying organized, as it allows you to assign tasks to other people, and free up your own time and energy to focus on more important tasks.
9. Communication - Effective communication is crucial for staying organized and efficient. This includes keeping in touch with your team, customers, and suppliers, and making sure that everyone is on the same page. It also includes using tools like email, instant messaging, and

project management software to stay connected and organized.
10. Review and evaluate - Regularly reviewing and evaluating your organizational and efficiency strategies can help you identify areas for improvement. This will allow you to make adjustments, optimize your strategies, and continuously improve your performance.

An example of how staying organized and efficient can lead to entrepreneurial success is a small business owner named Sarah who owns a clothing boutique. Sarah found herself struggling to keep up with her inventory, financial records, and customer information. She was also having trouble managing her time, and often found herself feeling overwhelmed and stressed out.

To address these issues, Sarah began implementing a number of organizational and efficiency strategies. She started by creating a schedule and prioritizing her tasks, focusing on the most important activities first. She also began using a CRM software and accounting software to keep track of her inventory, financial records, and customer information. Additionally, she implemented an automation system for her inventory management and financial record keeping.

By staying organized and efficient, Sarah was able to save time and energy and focus on growing her business. She began to attract more customers, and her sales and revenue started to increase. With the help of these tools, she also was able to streamline her business operation and was able to focus more on customer service. She also found that her stress levels decreased and she was more motivated to work on her business. By staying organized and efficient, Sarah was able to achieve greater success as an entrepreneur.

Staying organized and efficient is essential for entrepreneurial success. By following the key points outlined above, you can create an effective organizational structure, manage your time and tasks effectively, and focus on what is most important for your business. This will help you grow your business, achieve your goals, and ultimately become a successful entrepreneur.

CHAPTER 10 CONTINUOUSLY LEARNING AND ADAPTING

Entrepreneurship is an ever-evolving journey, and one of the keys to success is the ability to continuously learn and adapt. In this chapter, we will discuss the importance of staying informed and up-to-date on industry trends, as well as the strategies and techniques for implementing new knowledge and skills.

1. Stay informed about industry trends: Keeping up-to-date with the latest industry trends is crucial for staying competitive and identifying new opportunities. This can be done by subscribing to industry publications, attending conferences and networking events, and following thought leaders and influencers on social media.
2. Learn from others: Learning from others who have successfully navigated the entrepreneurial journey can provide valuable insights and strategies. This can be done by reading books and articles written by successful entrepreneurs, listening to podcasts, and attending mentorship programs.
3. Experiment and test new ideas: Entrepreneurship is all about taking risks and trying new things. It is important to be open to experimenting with new ideas and testing them out to see what works and what doesn't.
4. Continuously improve your skills: The more skills you have, the better equipped you will be to handle the challenges of entrepreneurship. Continuously improving your skills in areas such as marketing, finance, and management will give you a competitive edge and increase your chances of success.
5. Embrace change: In the fast-paced world of entrepreneurship, change is inevitable. Embracing

change and being open to new opportunities will help you stay ahead of the curve and navigate through the ups and downs of the entrepreneurial journey.
6. Seek feedback and constructive criticism: Regularly seeking feedback from customers, employees, and other stakeholders can provide valuable insights into areas of improvement and help you identify new opportunities. Additionally, being open to constructive criticism and using it to make necessary changes can help you continuously improve and adapt your business.
7. Invest in professional development: Investing in professional development opportunities such as training programs, workshops, and certifications can help you acquire new knowledge and skills that can be applied to your business.
8. Collaborate with others: Collaborating with other entrepreneurs, industry experts, and professionals can provide valuable perspectives and insights. Sharing ideas and working together can also help you come up with new and innovative solutions to problems.
9. Leverage technology: Technology is constantly evolving, and it is important to stay up-to-date with the latest tools and technologies that can improve your business operations and increase efficiency.
10. Stay curious: As an entrepreneur, it is important to always have a curious mindset. Being curious and asking questions can help you identify new opportunities, find solutions to problems, and learn from others.

Continuously learning and adapting is essential to the success of any entrepreneur. Staying informed about industry trends, learning from others, experimenting and testing new ideas, continuously improving your skills and embracing change are the key to continuously learning and adapting. These strategies will help you stay competitive and increase your chances of success in the ever-evolving world of entrepreneurship.

CHAPTER 11: SETTING AND ACHIEVING GOALS

Setting and achieving goals is crucial for entrepreneurial success. It helps to provide direction and focus, and allows you to measure your progress and success. Here are some key points to consider when setting and achieving goals as an entrepreneur:

1. Be specific: Your goals should be clear and specific, not vague or general. For example, instead of saying "I want to make more money," say "I want to increase my revenue by X% in the next quarter."
2. Make them measurable: Make sure your goals can be quantified and tracked, so you can measure your progress and know when you've achieved them.
3. Set deadlines: Give yourself a deadline for achieving each goal, so you stay motivated and on track.
4. Break them down: Break larger goals into smaller, more manageable steps. This will make them less daunting and easier to achieve.
5. Prioritize: Prioritize your goals and focus on the most important ones first.
6. Be realistic: Make sure your goals are realistic and achievable. It's important to have ambitious goals, but they should also be attainable.
7. Write them down: Write your goals down and post them where you can see them every day. This will help to keep them top of mind and remind you of what you're working towards.
8. Review and reassess: Regularly review and reassess your goals to make sure they're still relevant and aligned with your overall business strategy.
9. Celebrate your successes: Don't forget to celebrate your successes along the way, it is a way to keep you

motivated.
10. Learn from your failures: If you don't achieve a goal, don't be discouraged. Instead, use it as an opportunity to learn and make adjustments for the next time.
11. Get accountability partners: Surround yourself with people who will hold you accountable for achieving your goals. This can be a business partner, mentor, or accountability group. Having someone to report your progress to and receive feedback from can be very helpful in staying on track.
12. Use goal tracking tools: There are many goal tracking tools available such as Trello, Asana, and Evernote, that can help you to organize and track your progress. By using these tools, you can set reminders, create to-do lists, and track your progress in real-time.
13. Set long-term and short-term goals: As an entrepreneur, it's important to have both long-term and short-term goals. Long-term goals are objectives that you want to achieve over the next several years. Whereas, short-term goals are objectives that you want to achieve in the next few months. By setting both types of goals, you can make sure that you're always working towards something, and that you're not just focusing on the short-term.
14. Create actionable steps: Once you've set your goals, you'll need to create actionable steps to achieve them. These steps should be specific, measurable and have a deadline. By creating actionable steps, you'll be able to see what you need to do to achieve your goal, and you'll be able to track your progress.

By following these steps, you'll be able to set and achieve goals that are aligned with your overall business strategy, and that will help you to achieve your entrepreneurial aspirations.

Setting and achieving goals is an important aspect of entrepreneurial success. By being specific, measurable, and realistic, setting deadlines, breaking them down, prioritizing, and reviewing regularly, you'll be able to set and achieve goals that align with your overall business strategy and move closer to your entrepreneurial aspirations.

CHAPTER 12: BUILDING A STRONG TEAM

One of the most important aspects of entrepreneurial success is building and maintaining a strong team. A good team can help an entrepreneur achieve their goals, overcome obstacles, and drive the business forward. Here are some key points to keep in mind when building a strong team:

1. Hire the right people: The key to building a strong team is hiring the right people. Look for individuals who possess the skills and qualifications needed for the job, but also have the right personality and work ethic.
2. Clearly communicate expectations: It is important to clearly communicate expectations to team members from the start, so everyone is on the same page and understands their role and responsibilities.
3. Encourage collaboration and teamwork: Encourage team members to work together and collaborate on projects. This will help to build a sense of cohesion and unity among team members, which can lead to better performance and more effective problem-solving.
4. Recognize and reward good performance: Recognizing and rewarding good performance is essential for maintaining motivation and engagement among team members. This can be done through bonuses, promotions, or simply by giving verbal or written praise.
5. Provide opportunities for growth and development: Providing opportunities for growth and development is also important for maintaining motivation and engagement among team members. This can include training, mentoring, or opportunities for advancement within the company.
6. Encourage open communication: Encourage open

communication among team members and between team members and management. This will help to identify problems or issues early on, and to resolve them quickly and effectively.
7. Foster a positive work culture: Foster a positive work culture that values teamwork, respect, and communication. This will help to create a positive and supportive working environment, which can improve employee satisfaction, productivity and reduce turnover.
8. Empower team members: Give team members the autonomy and decision-making power they need to do their jobs effectively. This will help to build trust, increase motivation, and improve performance.
9. Lead by example: As a leader, it's important to lead by example and set a positive example for team members to follow. This includes being punctual, professional, respectful, and accountable.
10. Encourage diversity and inclusion: Encourage diversity and inclusion within your team. Having a diverse team can lead to better problem-solving, decision-making and creativity.
11. Use technology to collaborate: Utilize different tools like instant messaging, video conferencing, and project management software to help team members collaborate and stay on the same page, especially if team members are working remotely.
12. Manage conflicts effectively: Conflicts are bound to happen in any team. It's important to have a system in place to handle conflicts and address them in a timely and effective manner.
13. Continuously evaluate and improve: Continuously evaluate and improve the team's performance, processes and systems. This will help identify and address any issues, and make necessary adjustments to ensure the team is functioning as effectively and efficiently as

possible.

There are many important points to consider when building a strong team, here are a few additional ones that may be worth mentioning:

By following these steps, entrepreneurs can build and maintain a strong team that will help drive their business forward and achieve success. Remember that building a team takes time and effort, but the results are worth it. A strong team can help entrepreneurs overcome obstacles, achieve their goals and drive the business forward.

Building a strong team requires dedication, effective communication, and a willingness to adapt. By focusing on the points mentioned above and continuously evaluating and improving, entrepreneurs can build a team that will help drive their business forward and achieve success.

CHAPTER 13: DEVELOPING EFFECTIVE MARKETING STRATEGIES

Marketing is an essential aspect of any business and is crucial for the success of an entrepreneur. In this chapter, we will discuss the various marketing strategies that entrepreneurs can use to promote their products or services and reach their target market.

1. Define your target market: Before you can create an effective marketing strategy, you need to understand who your target market is. This includes identifying the demographics, needs, and pain points of your potential customers.
2. Understand your competition: It is important to research and understand your competition. Identify their strengths and weaknesses, and find ways to differentiate your products or services from theirs.
3. Develop a unique selling proposition (USP): A USP is a statement that clearly communicates the unique benefit of your product or service. It should be simple and easy to understand, and it should set you apart from your competitors.
4. Create a marketing mix: A marketing mix is a combination of different marketing strategies and tactics that you will use to reach your target market. This can include various forms of advertising, public relations, promotions, and sales.
5. Use social media: social media is a powerful tool for reaching a large audience at a low cost. Platforms like Facebook, Instagram, and Twitter can be used to connect with potential customers, share content, and generate leads.
6. Email marketing: Email marketing is a cost-effective and targeted way to reach potential customers. By

gathering email addresses from people who have shown interest in your products or services, you can send them targeted messages and promotions.

7. Influencer marketing: This strategy involves partnering with individuals who have a large and engaged following on social media. They can help promote your products or services to their audience.
8. Measure and evaluate: It is important to measure and evaluate the effectiveness of your marketing strategies. Use tools like Google Analytics to track website traffic and conversion rates, and use surveys and customer feedback to gather feedback on your marketing efforts.
9. Content marketing: Creating valuable and informative content such as blog posts, videos, and infographics can help attract and engage potential customers. By providing useful information, you can establish yourself as an authority in your industry and build trust with your target market.
10. Search engine optimization (SEO): SEO is the practice of optimizing your website and content to rank higher in search engine results. This can help increase visibility and drive more traffic to your website.
11. Paid advertising: Paid advertising can be an effective way to reach a larger audience quickly. Platforms like Google Ads and Facebook Ads allow you to create targeted campaigns and reach potential customers based on demographics and interests.
12. Public relations: Building relationships with journalists and media outlets can help increase visibility for your business. By developing a strong press release and pitching your story to relevant publications, you can increase brand awareness and generate media coverage.
13. Event marketing: Hosting events such as workshops, seminars, or networking events can be a great way to connect with potential customers and build relationships. By creating an engaging and memorable

experience, you can increase brand awareness and generate leads.

By following these steps and developing an effective marketing strategy, entrepreneurs can increase brand awareness, generate leads, and ultimately drive sales.

By utilizing a combination of these marketing strategies, entrepreneurs can create an effective marketing plan that reaches their target market and ultimately drives sales. It's important to regularly evaluate and adjust your marketing strategy as needed to ensure it is meeting your business goals.

CHAPTER 14: UNDERSTANDING AND COMPLYING WITH LEGAL AND REGULATORY REQUIREMENTS

One of the key steps to achieving entrepreneurial success is understanding and complying with the legal and regulatory requirements that apply to your business. Failure to do so can result in fines, penalties, and even legal action. Below are some key points to keep in mind when it comes to legal and regulatory compliance for your business:

1. Register your business: Depending on the type of business you are starting and the location, you may need to register your business with various government agencies. This can include registering with the state or local government, obtaining a business license, and registering for taxes.
2. Understand employment laws: As an employer, you are subject to a variety of laws and regulations related to the hiring, firing, and treatment of employees. This can include laws related to minimum wage, overtime pay, discrimination, and safety.
3. Familiarize yourself with intellectual property laws: If your business involves creating or using any type of creative work, such as music, writing, or software, you need to be familiar with laws related to copyright, trademark, and patents.
4. comply with industry-specific regulations: Depending on your industry, there may be specific regulations that you need to comply with. For example, if you are in the food industry, you will need to comply with food safety regulations, and if you are in the healthcare industry, you will need to comply with HIPAA regulations.

5. Have a plan for data protection: With the increasing amount of sensitive data being stored and shared electronically, it's crucial that business owners have a plan for data protection and compliance with data privacy regulations such as GDPR and CCPA.
6. Consult with a lawyer: Even if you are familiar with the legal and regulatory requirements that apply to your business, it is always a good idea to consult with a lawyer to ensure that you are in compliance and to help navigate any legal issues that may arise.
7. Keep accurate records: It is important to maintain accurate records of your business transactions, including all financial records, employee records, and any other records that are required by law. This will make it easier to comply with tax and other legal requirements, and will also help you to keep track of your business's performance over time.
8. Obtain necessary permits and licenses: Depending on the type of business you are running and the location, you may need to obtain various permits and licenses in order to operate legally. This can include permits for zoning, building, and health and safety.
9. Understand consumer protection laws: As a business, you are also subject to consumer protection laws that are designed to protect the rights of consumers. This can include laws related to advertising, product labelling, and warranties.
10. Comply with environmental laws: Many businesses are also subject to environmental regulations, which can include laws related to waste disposal, air and water pollution, and energy efficiency.

It's important to note that laws and regulations can change over time, so it's important to stay informed and keep up to date with any changes that may impact your business. Consulting with legal professionals, industry experts, and government agencies can be a great way to stay informed and ensure compliance.

Overall, understanding and complying with legal and regulatory requirements is an essential part of being a successful entrepreneur. By staying informed, staying compliant, and consulting with professionals as needed, you can help protect your business and ensure its long-term success.

CHAPTER 15: MANAGING RISK AND UNCERTAINTY

Entrepreneurship is inherently risky, and as a business owner, it's important to be able to identify and manage potential risks in order to ensure the success of your venture. In this chapter, we will explore strategies for managing risk and uncertainty in an entrepreneurial setting.

1. Identifying potential risks: The first step in managing risk is to identify the potential risks that your business may face. These can include economic downturns, changes in consumer preferences, legal and regulatory changes, and competition from other businesses.
2. Assessing the likelihood and impact of risks: Once you have identified potential risks, it's important to assess the likelihood of each risk occurring and the potential impact it could have on your business. This will help you prioritize which risks to focus on and how to address them.
3. Developing a risk management plan: Once you have assessed the risks, it's important to develop a plan to manage them. This may include developing contingencies and backup plans, implementing risk management procedures, and purchasing insurance.
4. Monitoring and reviewing risks: Even after you have implemented your risk management plan, it's important to monitor and review the risks facing your business on an ongoing basis, as the business environment is constantly changing. This will allow you to make adjustments to your plan as necessary.
5. Embracing uncertainty: While it's important to manage risks, it's also important to remember that uncertainty is a natural part of the entrepreneurial

process. Embracing uncertainty, being open to new opportunities, and learning from mistakes can help you become a more adaptable and resilient business owner.

6. Diversifying your business: Diversifying your business by having multiple streams of income and not putting all your eggs in one basket can also help mitigate risk and uncertainty.

7. Risk Mitigation: Risk mitigation is the process of reducing the likelihood or impact of a risk. This can be achieved through various methods such as implementing controls, transferring the risk to a third party, or accepting the risk. For example, if your business is at risk of a data breach, you can implement security controls such as firewalls, intrusion detection systems and encryption to reduce the likelihood of a breach. Another example is to transfer the risk by purchasing insurance to cover potential losses in case of a data breach.

8. Risk Management Software: There are many software programs available that can help you identify, assess, and manage risks. These software programs can automate the process of risk management, making it easier to keep track of risks, assign tasks and deadlines, and monitor progress. These software tools can also help in analysing data and identifying patterns which can be useful for forecasting and decision-making.

9. Risk Culture: Creating a risk-aware culture within your organization can help to ensure that risks are identified and managed effectively. This includes educating employees about risks, encouraging them to report risks, and rewarding them for identifying and managing risks. A risk-aware culture can also help to create a sense of accountability and ownership among employees, which can lead to a more efficient and effective risk management process.

Identifying potential risks: The process of identifying potential risks involves looking at all aspects of your business, including operations, finances, legal and regulatory requirements, and external factors such as the economy and competition. To identify potential risks, you can use tools such as a SWOT analysis, which looks at the strengths, weaknesses, opportunities, and threats facing your business.

Assessing the likelihood and impact of risks: Once you have identified potential risks, it's important to assess the likelihood of each risk occurring and the potential impact it could have on your business. This will help you prioritize which risks to focus on and how to address them. For example, a risk that has a high likelihood of occurring but a low impact on your business may not be as pressing to address as a risk that has a low likelihood of occurring but a high impact.

Developing a risk management plan: Once you have assessed the risks, it's important to develop a plan to manage them. This may include developing contingencies and backup plans, implementing risk management procedures, and purchasing insurance. For example, if your business is reliant on a single supplier, you might consider diversifying your supplier base to minimize the risk of supply chain disruptions. Another example is to have a disaster recovery plan in place in case of unexpected events like natural disasters, cyber-attacks, or power outages.

Monitoring and reviewing risks: Even after you have implemented your risk management plan, it's important to monitor and review the risks facing your business on an ongoing basis, as the business environment is constantly changing. This will allow you to make adjustments to your plan as necessary. This also includes being aware of the market changes and any new laws and regulations that may affect your business.

Embracing uncertainty: As an entrepreneur, you need to be prepared for the unexpected. While it's important to manage risks, it's also important to remember that uncertainty is a natural part of the entrepreneurial process. Embracing uncertainty, being open to new opportunities, and learning from mistakes can help you become a more adaptable and resilient business owner. This also means being open to pivoting your business model or entering new markets if your current one is not working out.

Diversifying your business: Diversifying your business by having multiple streams of income and not putting all your eggs in one basket can also help mitigate risk and uncertainty. This can be achieved by diversifying your product or service offerings, or exploring new revenue streams such as franchising, licensing, or e-commerce. Diversifying also includes having multiple customers and not relying on one major customer for the majority of your revenue.

Managing risk and uncertainty is an ongoing process that requires a proactive approach. By identifying, assessing, developing a plan, monitoring and reviewing risks, embracing uncertainty, diversifying, implementing risk mitigation and having a risk culture, you will be better equipped to navigate the inherent uncertainty of entrepreneurship and increase the chances of success.

CHAPTER 16: LEVERAGING TECHNOLOGY AND AUTOMATION

Technology and automation can play a significant role in the success of an entrepreneurial venture. By taking advantage of the latest tools and technologies, entrepreneurs can streamline their operations, increase efficiency, and improve their overall competitiveness. In this chapter, we will explore some key ways that entrepreneurs can leverage technology and automation to achieve success.

1. Automating repetitive tasks: By using automation tools and software, entrepreneurs can automate repetitive tasks, such as data entry and scheduling, freeing up valuable time and energy for more important tasks.
2. Utilizing social media and digital marketing: With the rise of the internet and social media, entrepreneurs can take advantage of these platforms to reach potential customers and build a strong online presence. Automation tools can also help to schedule and manage social media content and track analytics.
3. Implementing cloud-based tools and services: Cloud-based tools and services can help entrepreneurs to access their data and work remotely, as well as collaborate with team members in real-time.
4. Utilizing big data and analytics: Big data and analytics can help entrepreneurs to gain insights into customer behaviour and preferences, allowing them to make data-driven decisions and improve their marketing strategies.
5. Investing in e-commerce platforms: E-commerce platforms such as Amazon, Shopify, and others can help entrepreneurs to expand their reach and sell their products and services online.

6. Utilizing digital payment and financial management tools: Digital payment and financial management tools can help entrepreneurs to manage their finances more efficiently and securely.
7. Implementing customer relationship management (CRM) software: CRM software can help entrepreneurs to manage their customer relationships, track sales and customer interactions, and improve customer service.
8. Utilizing project management software: Project management software can help entrepreneurs to organize, plan and manage projects, assign tasks, and track progress. This can help to improve productivity and ensure that projects are completed on time and within budget.
9. Implementing inventory management software: Inventory management software can help entrepreneurs to track inventory levels, manage stock, and optimize inventory replenishment. This can help to improve inventory efficiency and reduce the risk of stockouts.
10. Utilizing supply chain management software: Supply chain management software can help entrepreneurs to manage the flow of goods and services, plan production, and track suppliers and logistics. This can help to improve the efficiency of the supply chain and reduce costs.
11. Implementing enterprise resource planning (ERP) systems: ERP systems can help entrepreneurs to integrate different business processes and systems, such as accounting, inventory management, and customer management. This can help to improve the overall efficiency and effectiveness of the business.
12. Utilizing artificial intelligence and machine learning: Artificial intelligence and machine learning can help entrepreneurs to automate decision-making, predict customer behaviour, and optimize business processes.

This can help to improve the overall performance of the business and create new opportunities.

Entrepreneurs who leverage technology and automation can improve their efficiency, productivity, and competitiveness. By utilizing automation tools, digital marketing and e-commerce platforms, big data and analytics, digital payment and financial management tools, CRM software, project management software, inventory management software, supply chain management software, ERP systems, and artificial intelligence and machine learning, entrepreneurs can gain a competitive edge and achieve success.

CHAPTER 17: LEVERAGING TECHNOLOGY AND AUTOMATION

In today's fast-paced and ever-changing business landscape, entrepreneurs need to stay ahead of the curve in order to be successful. One way to do this is by leveraging technology and automation to streamline processes, increase efficiency, and reduce costs.

1. Automating repetitive tasks: By using software and tools to automate repetitive tasks such as data entry, scheduling, and email marketing, entrepreneurs can free up valuable time and resources to focus on more important aspects of their business.
2. Using data analytics: By collecting and analysing data, entrepreneurs can gain valuable insights into their business operations, customers, and market trends. This information can then be used to make more informed decisions and improve overall performance.
3. Implementing cloud-based systems: Cloud-based systems such as CRM and accounting software allow entrepreneurs to access and manage their business data from anywhere at any time, making it easier to stay connected and collaborate with team members.
4. Utilizing social media and digital marketing: Social media and digital marketing platforms can be used to reach a wider audience, build brand awareness, and engage with customers in real-time.
5. Implementing e-commerce solutions: E-commerce solutions such as online stores and payment systems make it easy for entrepreneurs to sell products and services online and reach a global audience.
6. Investing in cybersecurity: As the number of cyber threats increases, it is important for entrepreneurs

to invest in cybersecurity measures such as firewalls and encryption to protect their business data and reputation.
7. Implementing project management software: Project management software can help entrepreneurs keep track of tasks, deadlines, and progress, making it easier to stay organized and on top of projects.
8. Utilizing virtual meeting tools: With the rise of remote work, virtual meeting tools such as Zoom, Skype, and Google Meet have become increasingly important for entrepreneurs to stay connected with team members, clients, and partners.
9. Investing in AI and machine learning: Artificial intelligence (AI) and machine learning (ML) technologies have the potential to revolutionize a variety of industries, from healthcare to finance. Entrepreneurs who invest in these technologies can gain a competitive advantage by automating processes and making data-driven decisions.
10. Optimizing website and mobile app design: Having a well-designed and user-friendly website or mobile app can improve customer experience and increase conversions. Entrepreneurs should invest in web and app development to ensure they are providing a seamless experience to their customers.
11. Utilizing automation in customer service: Automation in customer service can help entrepreneurs provide quick and efficient support to their customers, while also reducing the workload on human customer service agents.

By leveraging technology and automation, entrepreneurs can improve efficiency, reduce costs, and gain a competitive advantage in the marketplace. However, it is important to note that as technology changes, so must the entrepreneur's approach. Entrepreneurs need to continuously educate themselves on the latest advancements and update their strategies accordingly.

To elaborate further, one key benefit of leveraging technology and automation is that it can help entrepreneurs save time and resources. Automating repetitive tasks such as data entry, scheduling, and email marketing, for example, can free up valuable time and resources that can be used to focus on more important aspects of the business. This can also help to reduce human error and increase accuracy in these tasks.

Another key benefit is that technology and automation can help entrepreneurs gather and analyse data, providing valuable insights into their business operations, customers, and market trends. This information can then be used to make more informed decisions and improve overall performance. For example, using data analytics tools, an entrepreneur can track website traffic and customer behaviour to identify which products or services are most popular and where improvements are needed.

Cloud-based systems, such as CRM and accounting software, can also provide entrepreneurs with the flexibility to access and manage their business data from anywhere at any time, making it easier to stay connected and collaborate with team members. Similarly, e-commerce solutions such as online stores and payment systems make it easy for entrepreneurs to sell products and services online and reach a global audience.

In addition, leveraging technology and automation can also help entrepreneurs improve customer engagement and experience. Utilizing social media and digital marketing platforms can be used to reach a wider audience, build brand awareness, and engage with customers in real-time. Automation in customer service can help entrepreneurs provide quick and efficient support to their customers, while also reducing the workload on human customer service agents.

It's also important to note that investing in cybersecurity measures such as firewalls and encryption to protect their business data and reputation is crucial. With the number of cyber threats increasing, entrepreneurs must make sure they are protected against potential security breaches.

Leveraging technology and automation can provide entrepreneurs with a number of benefits, including saving time and resources, gaining valuable insights, improving efficiency and customer engagement, and protecting their business against cyber threats. It's important for entrepreneurs to stay up-to-date with the latest advancements and continuously adapt their strategies to stay ahead of the competition.

CHAPTER 18: MEASURING AND EVALUATING SUCCESS AND PROGRESS

Entrepreneurial success is not a destination, but a journey. It is important for entrepreneurs to continuously measure and evaluate their progress in order to identify areas for improvement and make necessary adjustments. In this chapter, we will discuss the importance of regularly measuring and evaluating success and progress, and provide some tips on how to effectively do so.

1. Set clear, measurable goals: Setting clear, measurable goals is the first step in evaluating success and progress. By setting specific, measurable goals, entrepreneurs can track their progress and determine if they are on track to achieving their objectives.
2. Regularly review progress: Regularly reviewing progress is crucial for identifying areas for improvement. This can be done through regular meetings with employees, monitoring financial reports, and analysing customer feedback.
3. Use key performance indicators (KPIs): Key performance indicators (KPIs) are specific, measurable values that can be used to track performance. Examples of KPIs for a business might include website traffic, sales numbers, or customer satisfaction scores.
4. Compare to industry benchmarks: It is also important to compare performance to industry benchmarks. This will give entrepreneurs a better understanding of how their business is performing in comparison to other businesses in the same industry.
5. Get feedback from customers and employees: Feedback from customers and employees can provide valuable insights into how a business is performing. Entrepreneurs should regularly solicit feedback and use

it to make improvements.
6. Reflect on lessons learned: Entrepreneurs should take time to reflect on the lessons they have learned from their experiences, both successes and failures. These lessons can be used to make better decisions in the future.
7. Celebrate successes: Finally, it is important for entrepreneurs to celebrate their successes. This not only helps to maintain motivation, but it also helps to build a positive culture within the organization.

Measuring and evaluating success and progress is an ongoing process that requires regular attention. By setting clear, measurable goals, regularly reviewing progress, using KPIs, comparing to industry benchmarks, getting feedback from customers and employees, reflecting on lessons learned, and celebrating successes, entrepreneurs can ensure that they are on track to achieving their objectives and making their business a success.

8. Use analytics tools: There are many tools available today that can help entrepreneurs track and analyse data related to their business. These tools can provide valuable insights into customer behaviour, website traffic, and sales trends. Entrepreneurs should consider using these tools to help them measure and evaluate success and progress.
9. Utilize A/B testing: A/B testing is a method of comparing two versions of a product or marketing campaign to determine which one is more effective. Entrepreneurs can use A/B testing to determine which marketing strategies are most effective, which website layouts are most user-friendly, or which product features are most popular.
10. Regularly review business plan: Entrepreneurs should regularly review their business plan to ensure that they are still on track to achieve their goals. Reviewing the

business plan can also help identify areas where changes are needed.

11. Monitor cash flow: Cash flow is critical for a business, and entrepreneurs should regularly monitor their cash flow to ensure that they have enough money to meet their financial obligations. This can help prevent financial problems down the road.
12. Review competitor activities: It is also important to keep an eye on what your competitors are doing. This can help entrepreneurs identify new opportunities and trends, and make adjustments to their own strategies as necessary.

Measuring and evaluating success and progress is a crucial aspect of being an entrepreneur. By following the steps outlined in this chapter, entrepreneurs can ensure that they are on track to achieve their goals and make necessary adjustments when needed.

One of the key steps to measuring and evaluating success is to regularly monitor and measure progress. This can be done by setting specific, measurable, achievable, relevant, and time-bound (SMART) goals and tracking progress towards those goals over time.

Entrepreneurs can also utilize analytical tools, such as financial statements and performance metrics, to assess the overall health and performance of their business. These tools can help identify areas of strength and weakness, as well as opportunities for growth and improvement.

Getting feedback from customers, employees, and other stakeholders is another important step in measuring and evaluating success. By gathering feedback and insights, entrepreneurs can better understand the needs and preferences of their target audience, identify areas for improvement, and make informed decisions about the direction of their business.

Celebrating successes and reflecting on lessons learned is also crucial for measuring and evaluating success. Celebrating successes can help build momentum and motivation, while reflecting on lessons learned can help entrepreneurs identify what worked well and what can be improved in the future.

Overall, measuring and evaluating success is an ongoing process that requires a commitment to continuous improvement and learning. By following these steps, entrepreneurs can ensure that they are on the right track to achieving their goals and building a successful business.

BONUS POINT

1

In order to commence a successful business venture, it is paramount to adhere to a set of important steps. The following guidelines will assist entrepreneurs in establishing and sustaining their business effectively.

Foremost, conducting comprehensive research on the target market is imperative. Gaining an in-depth understanding of the target audience's requirements, preferences, and pain points is critical in creating a product or service that caters to their demands. Such knowledge will enable entrepreneurs to tailor their offerings to the needs of their consumers, ultimately resulting in increased customer satisfaction and loyalty.

Developing a well-crafted business plan is also vital to the success of any enterprise. The plan should encompass the company's objectives, target market, marketing strategies, financial projections, and other significant details. This blueprint facilitates entrepreneurs in staying organized and focused on their goals.

Another critical factor in establishing a thriving business is providing exceptional customer service. Customers are the backbone of any business, and providing top-notch service can distinguish a business from its competitors. Entrepreneurs should be receptive to customer feedback, inquiries, and concerns and strive to exceed their expectations.

Building a robust brand identity is also crucial. A strong brand reflects the company's values, personality, and vision. Investing in a good logo, website, and social media presence can assist entrepreneurs in establishing a distinct identity in a crowded market.

Technology is another indispensable aspect of modern business. Utilizing technology to automate processes, streamline operations, and reach customers more efficiently can significantly enhance a business's success.

It is equally essential to be adaptable in the ever-changing business world. Entrepreneurs should be open to new ideas, willing to pivot when necessary, and learn from their mistakes.

Effective financial management is critical to the success of any business. Accurate record-keeping, managing cash flow, and investing in tools and resources are all necessary components of successful financial management.

Networking is a valuable tool for entrepreneurs to build relationships, find new customers, and gain valuable insights into their industry. Attending events, joining industry groups, and utilizing social media can all help entrepreneurs connect with others in their field.

Lastly, hiring the right people is crucial. Employees are a reflection of the company, and hiring individuals who share the same values, possess relevant experience, and are passionate about the industry can significantly contribute to the success of the business.

By following these guidelines, entrepreneurs can establish a successful business that thrives in a competitive market. It is essential to stay focused on the core business, adapt to changes, and continuously strive for excellence in all aspects of the enterprise.

2

Knowing your potential customers is essential for any successful business. In order to effectively market your products or services, you need to have a deep understanding of who your customers are, what they need, and what motivates them to make a purchase. In this article, we will delve into who your potential customers are and how you can connect with them.

Demographic Information

The first step to understanding your potential customers is to collect their demographic information. This includes their age, gender, income level, education level, and location. This information helps you create buyer personas, which are representations of your ideal customers.

Age and Gender

Your target audience's age and gender will vary depending on your industry and the products or services you offer. For example, if you're selling beauty products, your primary target audience may be females aged 18 to 35. But if you're selling financial services, your target audience may be both males and females between the ages of 30 and 60.

Income and Education Level

Knowing your target audience's income and education level is crucial for creating effective marketing campaigns. If you're selling luxury goods or services, your target audience may belong to a higher income bracket. However, if you're selling everyday items or services, your target audience may come from a wider range of income levels.

Location

Your target audience's location is also important to consider. If you have a physical store, you may be targeting customers within a certain radius of your location. But if you have an online store, your target audience could be located anywhere in the world.

Interests and Hobbies

Besides demographic information, it's important to understand your potential customers' interests and hobbies. This information helps you tailor your marketing efforts to appeal to their specific interests and hobbies. For example, if you're selling outdoor gear, your target audience may be interested in hiking, camping, and other outdoor activities.

Pain Points and Needs

Understanding the pain points and needs of your potential customers is also crucial. By knowing what problems they're trying to solve or what needs they have, you can tailor your marketing efforts to provide solutions that meet those needs. For example, if you're selling skincare products, your target audience may be looking for solutions to acne, dry skin, or other skin issues.

Motivations for Making a Purchase

Finally, understanding what motivates your potential customers to make a purchase is key to creating successful marketing campaigns. This could be anything from a desire for convenience to a desire for luxury. By knowing these motivations, you can tailor your marketing efforts to speak directly to those desires.

Knowing your potential customers is vital to the success of

your business. By collecting and analyzing their demographic information, interests and hobbies, pain points and needs, and motivations for making a purchase, you can tailor your marketing efforts to reach the right audience and connect with them. Effective marketing is all about creating a connection with your customers and showing them that you understand their needs.

3

Setting clear, measurable goals is the first step in evaluating success and progress. It is essential for entrepreneurs to have a plan in place to monitor progress and make data-driven decisions. In this article, we will discuss six essential steps to help entrepreneurs evaluate their success and progress.

Set specific, measurable goals
The first step to evaluating success and progress is to set specific, measurable goals. Entrepreneurs should establish goals that are specific and achievable. This helps to create a clear path for success and enables them to measure their progress. Setting measurable goals provides a tangible way to track progress, enabling entrepreneurs to make data-driven decisions.

Regularly review progress
Entrepreneurs must regularly review their progress to identify areas for improvement. This can be done through regular meetings with employees, monitoring financial reports, and analyzing customer feedback. Regular progress reviews allow entrepreneurs to identify any areas of the business that require improvement and implement strategies to address these areas.

Use key performance indicators (KPIs)
Key performance indicators (KPIs) are specific, measurable values that can be used to track performance. KPIs provide valuable

insights into the success of a business. Examples of KPIs for a business might include website traffic, sales numbers, or customer satisfaction scores. By regularly tracking KPIs, entrepreneurs can gain a deeper understanding of their business's performance and make data-driven decisions.

Compare to industry benchmarks
It is essential to compare performance to industry benchmarks. This enables entrepreneurs to gain a better understanding of how their business is performing in comparison to other businesses in the same industry. By comparing performance to industry benchmarks, entrepreneurs can identify areas for improvement and make data-driven decisions to address any deficiencies.

Get feedback from customers and employees
Feedback from customers and employees can provide valuable insights into how a business is performing. Entrepreneurs should regularly solicit feedback and use it to make improvements. Feedback can be collected through surveys, focus groups, or one-on-one conversations. This information can be used to identify areas of the business that require improvement and implement strategies to address these areas.

Reflect on lessons learned
Entrepreneurs should take time to reflect on the lessons they have learned from their experiences, both successes and failures. These lessons can be used to make better decisions in the future. Reflecting on past experiences can provide valuable insights into the business and enable entrepreneurs to make informed decisions.

Celebrate successes
Finally, it is essential for entrepreneurs to celebrate their successes. Celebrating successes not only helps to maintain motivation but also helps to build a positive culture within the organization. This positive culture can motivate employees to

continue to strive for success and can contribute to the long-term success of the business.

Setting clear, measurable goals is the first step in evaluating success and progress. By following these six essential steps, entrepreneurs can track their progress, identify areas for improvement, and make data-driven decisions to achieve their objectives. Regularly reviewing progress, using KPIs, comparing performance to industry benchmarks, soliciting feedback, reflecting on lessons learned, and celebrating successes are critical components of evaluating success and progress in business.

SUMMARY

Entrepreneurial Success: the 18 great step to Entrepreneurial Success is a guide that covers the key steps to achieving success as an entrepreneur. It includes topics such as developing a clear business plan, identifying target market, networking, market research, finding funding, building a strong brand, hiring and managing employees, managing finances, staying organized, continuously learning, setting and achieving goals, building a strong team, developing effective marketing strategies, understanding legal and regulatory requirements, managing risk, leveraging technology, maintaining a positive mindset, and measuring and evaluating success. The guide aims to provide entrepreneurs with the tools and strategies they need to start and grow a successful business.

Additionally, the guide focuses on providing practical and actionable advice for entrepreneurs at all stages of their business journey. It covers essential topics such as developing a business plan, identifying target market, networking, market research, finding funding, building a strong brand, hiring and managing employees, managing finances, staying organized, continuously learning, setting and achieving goals, building a strong team, developing effective marketing strategies, understanding legal and regulatory requirements, managing risk, leveraging technology, maintaining a positive mindset, and measuring and evaluating success. The guide is designed to be a comprehensive resource that can be used by entrepreneurs of all experience levels, from those just starting out to those who are looking to take their business to the next level.

Furthermore, the guide also covers the importance of maintaining a positive attitude and mindset throughout the entrepreneurial journey. Starting a business can be a challenging and stressful process, and it's essential to keep a positive attitude and stay motivated. The guide also includes information on how to manage risk and uncertainty, which is an inevitable part of starting and growing a business. The guide provides valuable insights on how to manage finances, cash flow, and evaluate progress and success. The guide also highlights the importance of staying on top of legal and regulatory requirements. It can be overwhelming for entrepreneurs to navigate the legal side of starting a business, but this guide provides practical advice on how to stay compliant and avoid any legal issues.

Overall, Entrepreneurial Success: the 18 great step to Entrepreneurial Success is an invaluable resource for anyone looking to start or grow a business. It covers all the key steps and strategies that entrepreneurs need to know to be successful and provides practical, actionable advice that can be implemented immediately.

ABOUT THE AUTHOR

Emmanuel Amagada

Emmanuel Amagada is an author on the rise, carving out a niche in the self-help genre. With a passion for the written word that burns brightly, he has honed his craft to create a unique style that captivates readers and holds their attention with ease. His writing is characterized by its directness, clarity, and penetrating insights, drawing readers in with every turn of phrase.

But don't let the simplicity of his words fool you – there is a depth to Emmanuel's writing that belies its apparent ease. His sentences are carefully crafted, each one containing layers of meaning that reveal themselves upon closer inspection. From the shortest, punchiest statements to the longer, more complex sentences that unfurl like ribbons, Emmanuel's writing is a study in variation and balance.

Whether he is offering practical advice for overcoming obstacles in life or delving into the mysteries of the human psyche, Emmanuel's prose is never dull or predictable. Instead, it is a masterful blend of simplicity and complexity, a testament to the power of words to inspire, inform, and transform.

BOOKS BY THIS AUTHOR

The Art Of Deception: Recognizing And Dealing With The Lies Of Cheaters In Relationships

"The Art of Deception: Recognizing and Dealing with the Lies of Cheaters in Relationships" is a practical guide for anyone who has experienced infidelity or dishonesty in their romantic relationships. The book offers insights into the psychology of cheaters and the common techniques they use to deceive their partners, as well as practical advice and strategies for recognizing and dealing with their lies.

The book covers a range of topics, including how to confront a cheater, deciding whether to stay or leave the relationship, setting healthy boundaries, rebuilding trust, and seeking therapy and support. It also includes real-life case studies and examples of how individuals have handled infidelity and deception, as well as strategies for preventing future cheating and promoting healthy communication and honesty in all relationships.

Whether you are currently dealing with infidelity in your relationship or simply want to learn more about the art of deception, "The Art of Deception" provides valuable insights and practical tools for recognizing and dealing with the lies of cheaters in relationships.

The Root Causes Of Infidelity: Understanding And Preventing Cheating In Relationships

This book explores the complex and emotional topic of infidelity in relationships. It provides insights into the causes and consequences of infidelity, as well as practical advice on how to prevent, cope with, and recover from infidelity. The book emphasizes the importance of effective communication, emotional intimacy, and trust in maintaining healthy and fulfilling relationships. It also delves into the impact of societal and cultural factors on infidelity, and offers guidance on how to address the emotional toll on children affected by infidelity. Overall, the book provides a comprehensive and compassionate guide for individuals and couples seeking to navigate the challenges of infidelity in their relationships.

Navigating The Complexities Of Modern Relationships: A Guide To Building And Maintaining Healthy

Navigating the complexities of modern relationships is a guide to building and maintaining healthy connections with others. This guide covers a variety of topics, including effective communication, trust and honesty, emotional intelligence, conflict resolution, self-care and boundaries, emotional support and intimacy, relationship styles, the impact of technology and social media, understanding and managing expectations, navigating change and growth, forgiveness and moving on, cultural and societal influences, relationship counseling and therapy, building a stronger relationship, and self-awareness and self-reflection. The goal of this guide is to provide individuals with the tools and knowledge they need to build and maintain strong, healthy, and fulfilling relationships with others. By incorporating these principles and practices into your relationships, you can create connections that are built on trust, respect, and mutual understanding.